The Principles of Netiquette
By David Chiles

The Principles of Netiquette
By David Chiles
Second Edition

The Principles of Netiquette

Published by David Paul Chiles

Edition: 2016

For Everyone!

Table of Contents

This is the second edition of the Principles of Netiquette. Revised specifically to address feedback and updates to the site NetworkEtiquette.net. A MOOC offered by Duke University through Coursera was taken to make the writing more cohesive. Engagement from online works since taking writing, ethics, and social media courses is the guide for using writing techniques to create a more engaging book.

Introduction

This is a textbook for everyone. Comfortable use of the internet is the intended outcome from reading it. Fundamental use is at the core of each chapter. Historic achievements in technology are included to give usage context. Acceptable, popular use, is explained as a conclusion. Everything is based on the Golden Rule.

Chapter 1 Introduction to Netiquette

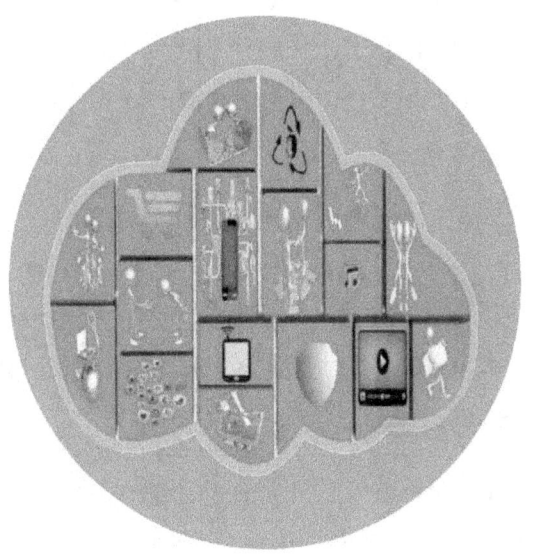

"Treat others the way you want to be treated."

Humanity follows this socially conscious principle to build societies. Netiquette is the Golden Rule's application to create Internet Society. It builds comfort in social interaction with a conscious effort of inclusion in our actions since we must consider what others may think.

A principle is a fundamental truth, law, rule, guideline, moral, or ethic used to form a system of beliefs that influence behavior in society. A way of thinking. Agreement on them creates societies.

Common knowledge is the community standard. Society is all the relationships between people living in a defined community. Intellectual expressions are the culture.

Internet Society is the communication between us around the world because engagement is a relationship and the internet is all over the world. Netiquette is the common knowledge, order, of the online community. The culture is the content we consume, intellectual property.

The principles of netiquette are the Golden Rule, government laws, rules, guidelines, morals, and ethics of computer communication. Social standards that influence online conduct are the rules and guidelines, netiquette.

Netiquette

Communication is cultural. We read, watch, listen, create, and share intellectual property. Consumption is the culture. The community is growing with every transmission.

Network etiquette is the culture of the internet because intellectual property is the communication. The expressions we share define the community. Rules are the common conventions.

Conventional conduct is proper. This is central to the community. There is more or less appropriate interaction.

Definition

Netiquette is the social code of network communication. A moral code for effective communication through the Internet based on the 'Human Condition' and Golden Rule. A public policy document stating the mission and intent of an organizations engagement.

The word was created by combining network and etiquette. It is a portmanteau. The combination of two words.

A computer network is a collection of computers that use digital communication. Binary code is a series of electric pulses that represent the digits 1 and 0. It is interpreted and displayed on screens or played through speakers.

Etiquette is a social code of behavior according to conventional standards. The popular way of doing things. Therefore, netiquette is the social code of the internet because the internet is a computer network and etiquette is a social code.

Rules

The rules of netiquette are cultural norms. They are based on computer networking techniques. Social influences regulate our behavior.

Popular use creates conventional wisdom. These conventions become common knowledge. Hence, they are the social standards we follow.

Social guidelines influence the way we act. Education plays a key role because internet use has to be taught since it is highly technical. Furthermore, it changes rapidly with technology. Continuing education is a social principle because of rapidly changing technology.

Policy

The Golden Rule is the fundamental truth. Laws set the boundary for the lowest possible acceptable behavior. Rules and guidelines are a matter of policy for a given community. Morals represent the ethical nature of the code.

Many countries, companies, and cities have netiquette policies linked to their social media accounts and websites. These documents influence users more or less depending on contacts. They serve as a guide without force in an ethical context.

Netiquette is based on the Golden Rule as ethics for the online community at the highest level. A document stating the rules or moral intent is a central component. Laws are beneath the system of beliefs.

History

The word netiquette was created the same year as the word internet, 1982. Adherence to cultural conventions emerged when we shared information. It began immediately because it is natural.

1969 1st Transmission

1971 Email

1982 Newsgroups

1984 Domain Name System (DNS)

1985 Websites

2006 NetworkEtiquette.net

The University of California at Los Angeles (UCLA) first created internet technology. College students made the first transmission in 1969. A professor's research paper on packet switching technology was the basis of the technology.

Kleinrock, a professor, supervised a student attempt a login to a remote computer from UCLA to Stanford. 'l' and 'o' were transmitted. The terminal crashed when thc 'g' was input.

Email was the first application. The software was developed in 1971 to send computer messages as an alternative to the telephone. It was designed with the @ symbol as the network identifier.

Internet newsgroups began in 1982 using forum software. These are first generation websites, web 1.0. Users post articles. They connect to a remote computer and download a file to a local computer. The word netiquette was first written in a humorous post on November 15, 1982.

HyperText Markup Language (HTML) was created from Standard Generalized Markup Language (SGML) in 1984. It enabled web pages to connect to each other with hyperlinks. Symbolics.com was the first website registered March 15, 1985.

This was the second generation, Web 2.0. It includes information production and interactive participation in addition to downloading files. JavaScript, database access, and templates made dynamic web pages possible.

Netiquette is defined by NetworkEtiquette.net registered in 2006. South Korea began teaching the subject. Web 3.0 is adaptive. Cellular telephones begin using the Internet. Information extraction influences layout and presentation.

Web 4.0 is Self-Monitoring Analysis and Reporting Technology (SMART). Apps provide information we use to make decisions. Wearables monitor vital signs and track movement.

Principles

Principles govern everything we do consciously. Consciousness requires education, religion, or both. Uneducated people without religion are not conscious.

Beliefs must be taught. Some people do not know any better. Propositions serve as the basis for reasoning behavior. They influence our actions.

Social Media, Education, Business, E-mail, and Video are reasons we use the internet. Mobile is a method of communication. Safety practices are central to its use.

The Golden Rule is the underlying belief of social interaction. Also known as the rule of reciprocity. We exchange polite behavior with one another. Treat others as we want to be treated.

Societies form based on this principle. Schools are built on it. People learn from it. All knowledge has been acquired from systems based on its use. The internet is a product of it.

Common knowledge can be identified by quantifiable standards. Beliefs can be tested. When there is agreement in principle, standards can be measured.

The Golden Rule

Sharing knowledge makes us equal by giving us measurable standards to uphold. The rule of reciprocity brings us together because it creates an obligation to do something for others. It creates societies through sharing.

Reciprocity

Cicero is a famous Greek author whose work is used as placeholder text by web designers before content is added. He said, *"There is no duty more indispensable than that of returning kindness"*.

The Golden Rule, *'treat others the way you want to be treated'*, implies that others will treat you as you treat them. Being treated by others the way you treat them is reciprocal.

Reciprocity applies to the internet. A social duty exists to exchange compliments and constructive criticism. Compliments are kind words and other affirmations. Constructive criticism is complimentary advice.

Effective Communication

Effective communication, in principle, is short, sweet, and to the point. The Golden Rule defines understanding in the most basic sense. We must be conscious of the way we treat others.

Brevity, clarity, and ethics contribute to effective communication in a measurable way. Long messages are not well received. Information has to be clear for understanding. Lies invalidate a network. Without truth there is nothing.

Brevity

Brevity is used in principle by including necessary information only. Communication comes from posting. We use acronyms, link shorteners, and affirmations as a measure of this principle.

A lot of us click away from content if it takes too long to load. This is measured by the number of users who click away after visiting one page, Bounce Rate. Brevity is used to increase consumption.

Brief communication conveys few words. It is short. Acronyms are used to shorten text. Hyperlinks are shortened with software to take up less space. Affirmation is measured by various statistics.

Input in forms are part of the process on all levels. Navigation requires hyperlink input. Mobile accepts input in text boxes through popup touch screen keyboards or keys. Social media uses forms to post information for contacts.

Education uses forms in discussion forums, assignments, and testing. Safety can be observed by posting brief information. Forms collect customer data in business. Email requires address and message input. Video has description and comment forms.

Long posts receive little affirmation. Everything internet related is expected to be brief. Our navigation habits are measured to acquire this common knowledge. We expect the content to be short. If it takes too long, we find it elsewhere.

Acronyms

'Laugh out loud' is a popular expression. The acronym for it is popular culture. 'lol' can be heard on television and in music. It is proper netiquette because it is popular. We know what it means.

An acronym is a pronounced word created with the initial letters of a term or phrase. An abbreviation of words that forms a separate word shorter than the term. Proper netiquette for use depends on understanding.

If the audience understands acronyms they are effective. If you do not know your audiences understanding level, it is best to use whole words. More people will understand the content that way.

Link Shortener

The internet thrives on sharing hyperlinks. Search engines rank content from links to a site and how the content relates. Descriptive Universal Resource Locators (URL's) rank higher. The more descriptive, the longer it is.

Link shortener websites shorten long hyperlinks. They provide tracking analytics as well (See Appendix A for websites). The shortened link directs clicks to the original address.

Smaller links leave more room for a description. Descriptions of link content are influential to viewers and search engines. The analytics provided may be used for A/B Testing (See Chapter 7) or simple review. We can see how many people clicked on a link and where they came from.

Content

The internet is what we post on it. We engage data posted on servers. This includes the text in forms or other content of a website.

In principle, brief posts are engaged. Long posts are ignored. In practice, many networks limit the size of posts.

Users affirm brief posts in a measurable way on all levels. Clicking shortened hyperlinks over long ones is measurable. Short social posts are more liked and shared than long ones. Long mobile posts are difficult to compose.

Long coursework is not reviewed well by peers. Safety requires certain information be withheld. Business happens fast. Long input slows it down. Long emails are not read. Video shorts are preferred.

Clarity

Clarity is understanding with context. Standard language is used to be clear. Slang is ambiguous, unclear.

Clear communication is easily perceived. This is a quality of effective internet communication. Clarity is a principle.

An unambiguous message is clearly understood. Ambiguous information is open to interpretation. Interpretation depends on formal and informal education.

Understanding

Unclear information means different things to different people. We have our own understanding of it. Some people are not capable of comprehension at all.

This has to be taken into account. Understanding is clear when information is interpreted in a standard way. Common experiences and knowledge are good references for clarity. They convey understanding by example.

Explicit information is clearly stated with minimum education required to know what the surrounding words and background information mean. Implicit means logically inferred.

Context

Context is often a social construct of the intended recipient and the author. A message means what you think it means. Understanding requires a relationship built around the content for context.

The relationship of a word to the surrounding words, expressions, and other related data create context. The intent of the author is a part of it. Messages can easily be taken out of context if they are not clear.

We are taught how to reason in school. We learn how to get along with each other from our friends. Understanding depends on education and experience because school teaches common knowledge and friends experience things together.

Ambiguity

Ambiguous information is data that can reasonably be interpreted in various ways. Reasonable interpretation is based on education or experience. Guessing is unreasonable.

Words with multiple meanings can make a sentence ambiguous. Providing context can make them clear. Misunderstanding should be considered during composition.

Explicit knowledge is not ambiguous. Implicit knowledge is derived by logical deductions from available information. Clear information contains the elements defining its meaning explicitly or implicitly. Correct interpretation is effective communication.

Violence has erupted from a text message missing a word causing it to be taken out of context. This is an extreme example. In the most basic sense ambiguous information may require extra communication for understanding. It may never be completely understood.

Ethics

Ethics is understanding right from wrong. Knowing what is good, fair, and honest according to popular standards is the right.

Truth gives us the opportunity to make the right decisions. Lies enslave us because they leave little or no choice about our actions. Lying is wrong, bad, and unethical. Cheating is not fair. Stealing is dishonest.

False information has entertainment value because feelings are real. It is what it is. How it makes us feel when consumed.

Effective communication is ethical. The measurable nature of online communication promises to make the world fair and honest. It started as joke in 1982 when netiquette was created and the computer was named Time Magazines 'Man of The Year'. We are taking it seriously now. The Information Age has begun.

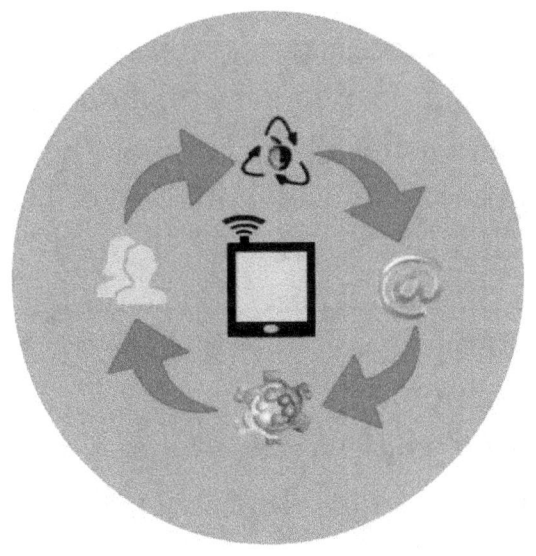

Etiquette is comfortability. It applies to the internet. Core rules are make communication comfortable in principle. Guidelines offer a range of conventional practices for online activities.

Core Rules

- Review messages because errors make communication hard to understand.
- Avoid using all caps to shout because the caps lock style of writing is for headings.
- Tell the truth providing vague statements if necessary to protect privacy because lies destroy the community.
- Be yourself, so the internet is taken seriously for all the good things it can do for society.
- Refrain from insulting others online because it is cyberbullying.
- Get approval before sending and ignore unsolicited messages because it is a costly security risk.

- Be conservative in messages you send and liberal in those you receive because sending messages is more personal than receiving relevant information.
- Send messages within an appropriate time based on the content of the message.
- Use secure websites when possible because encryption protects data from flaws in non-secure websites.
- Use discretion because data can easily be compromised.

Guidelines

Tabbed Browsing

Tabbed browsing increases the speed at which we navigate the internet. A web browser opens in a window. Within the browser window is a tab that displays content. Tabs align next to each other. The active tab is on top.

They open faster than browser windows. Opening a new window slows a computer down. Opening multiple windows can cause the computer to crash due to memory overload from too many processes.

There are keyboard shortcuts that can be used for tabbed browsing. Holding down the control button and clicking a hyperlink opens the link in a new tab. Holding down control and pressing "T" opens a blank tab. These shortcuts open faster than windows, perform better without the risk of crash, and save time by increased navigation speed.

Page Settings

Using custom browser settings by domain can save time navigating. Disable pop-ups on sites that display them for administrative features, login, and settings. When a message appears that a pop-up has been blocked from a click, change the settings. Then you will not have to allow it every time you visit.

Cache

Cache memory has a big effect on the browser speed and performance. It can be managed in the settings. Cache should be between 5% and 10% of total Ram. The more memory allocated to the cache, the better a browser will perform.

It can be manually cleared to increase speed and privacy. A full Cache memory operates slower than an empty one. Cookies and other private data is stored there. Clearing browser data deletes the cache.

We can do it after each time we use the browser for increased performance, security, and privacy. It deletes the history and saved login information. There is nothing saved in it to slow us down next time we use it.

Boolean Operators

Using Boolean Operators "AND", "OR", and "NOT" in search queries provides more relevant search results. The operators must be written in all caps. Using them is a way of thinking about the results you desire. This AND that. Either this OR that. NOT that.

The Boolean operator "AND" is a parameter that requires both conditions are satisfied for relevant results. It excludes results that do not have both conditions.

The Boolean operator "OR" is parameter that requires either condition is satisfied for relevant results. It does not exclude results with any of the terms on either side of the "OR".

The Boolean operator "NOT" is a search parameter that excludes results with the associated term.

Keywords

A keyword is a word or phrase used by search engines to find relevant content. They are query input. Research can save time, money, and better educate us by providing more relevant results.

We look until we find websites with the content we seek, which is time consuming. Products and services are purchased from searching at a cost. Information for education is sought to educate us. More relevant results improve everything.

Research tells us about relevant terms. Synonyms can be used to find content. Statistics regarding terms provide information that may be useful when deciding which ones to use. Large websites and search engines provide data on keywords for advertising and research purposes (See Appendix A for a list of keyword research websites).

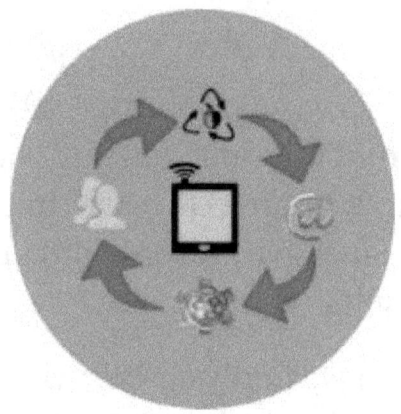

Internet Etiquette

Etiquette comes from common beliefs. The standards must be taught. It took three layers in principle to build the internet big enough for comfortable interaction between us to exist. Netiquette started as a joke in a newsgroup.

Now, it is the proper way we conduct ourselves online. A way that others are comfortable with. Fundamental uses are popular online activities. Enforcement of norms is determined by the influence of relationships.

We are moving toward a society that is based on internet use. Informatization is the transformation. Regular participation in these fundamental activities is the outcome.

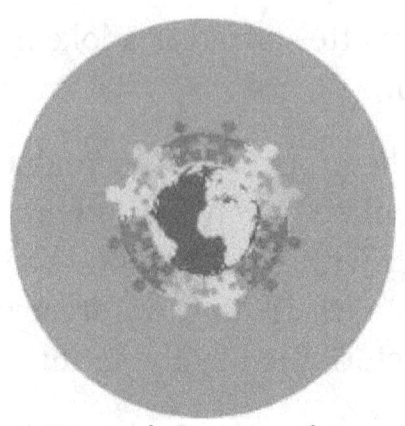

Digital Citizenship

Digital citizens inhabit the internet to communicate with each other. This exchange of information requires a connection. Therefore, you are not a digital citizen until and unless you establish a connection with others online.

Existence is a socially conscious state of usage. Connections have influence. There is a right to use the internet. It comes with responsibility. The Golden Rule creates the responsibility of reciprocity to connections.

Netiquette is all the expressions of the online community. Digital Citizenship is membership in it. We are recognized for our online image by connections. The internet is part of our daily lives.

Browser

We look at the internet through a software browser. Browse describes the activity of internet use. Browser describes a software program used to view content.

The fundamental routine of using the internet consists of browsing. Browsing is what we do. Engagement is what it enables.

Engage means to communicate. In practice we consume information online. We give our attention to others and their content for sharing information, communication.

The internet is a series of hyperlinks to content. Content can only be consumed through browsing because of its arrangement in hyperlinks. It is the core activity online communication.

Cookies

A cookie is a small text file inserted in browsers when we arrive at a site. The file allows sites to store and track unique information. Typically, they store login information and track the pages we visit.

Sites have to know who we are to give us access. Cookies provide this unique identification. They provide the ability to track us when they leave the site as well.

Clearing the cache as previously described deletes them. Some countries require notification of use. Others do not.

Search

A search engine is a software program. There are internet search engines and domain search engines. They supply relevant hyperlinks in response to queries.

The software provides a user interface for a relational database. The data inside is a collection of binary information indexed by rows and columns. It is an index of hyperlinks, metadata, text, and other content contained within a page.

The Search Engine Results Page (SERP) is the group of links provided by the application from a query. This page generally includes free and paid results. Free results are considered organic. The advertising links are Pay Per Click (PPC) 'sponsored' by content providers.

Organic search results are based on Relevancy. PPC ads appear above organic results on the most popular search websites. These sites have their own communities that center around services they provide (See Appendix A for a list of search engine websites).

VoIP

The internet can be used to talk. Voice, video, and chat are popular ways to talk to other people on the internet.

VoIP stands for Voice over Internet Protocol. A process of using the internet for telecommunications. The protocol identifies its data separately from other internet data. On some networks it is given preference by law.

Video conferencing and chat are included. It evolved from purely voice data to become a standard for synchronous communication. Real time connections with participants.

Video conferencing is a synchronized exchange of audio and video between participants. Video Chat is a form of video conferencing. It is a person to person talk through web cams with a specific app.

VoIP and Video Conferencing applications include chat and text options. They may allow synchronous or asynchronous text as well. Text chat is a person to person synchronized exchange of short messages. Generally, 140 characters or less.

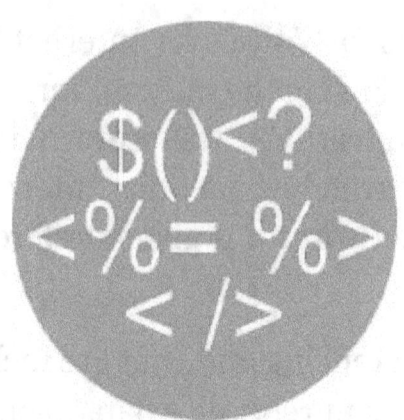

Web Design

A design is a plan or drawing. A good design requires a good plan. A good drawing contributes to a good plan.

HyperText Markup Language (HTML), Cascading Style Sheets (CSS), and JavaScript (js) are the principle programming languages for displaying data on the internet. PHP, Ruby, and jQuery are the most common programming languages for manipulating displayed data with database content. Oracle and Structured Query Language (SQL) are the languages used to extract data from databases.

HyperText Mark-Up Language (HTML) is a programming language created for hyperlinking data. It is object oriented. HTML tags are objects.

Cascading Style Sheets (CSS) allow programmers to format data between tags. CSS uses standard HTML as a basis for the techniques. Generally, this formatting technique creates a central place to control the style of a website. CSS files are style sheets.

JavaScript is an object oriented programming language that gives data functionality in the dynamics of how it is displayed. It is the code used to make buttons click, windows pop-up, and images appear when something on screen comes into focus. There are higher level languages built on it that have added functionality as well.

Activity

Browsing, searching, talking, and designing are categories for online activities. We do these things without thinking about them. All of them can be done with a smartphone. Most of us have one. So we are capable of becoming Digital Citizens.

Core services are provided through the internet. Utilities can be found online. They are things we need for everyday life and a type of software.

Electricity is a utility for life. Electronic communication is a utility app. Comfortable use of a web browser is more convenient at the most basic level because utilities are online. We are beginning to rely on the internet.

There is a lot of helpful information online. Most human knowledge can be found. The information may assist us in any activity. The higher quality of life online information provides is something we are becoming accustomed to.

VoIP uses less network resources than traditional telecommunications. Smartphones have VoIP apps. Network demand is increasing with our population. Using VoIP now is a growing trend. It may become necessary due to network limitations.

Websites make up our online image. A good design contributes to a good image. Knowing design techniques provides an understanding of how our data is displayed in online accounts. We make better profiles by understanding how data is displayed.

Daily internet use has become conventional. Websites provide core services and functions. Searching for information improves our lives. Talking on the phone may be done with an app. Designing the display of our data makes us look good.

It is informatization. Embrace it because it is happening. Let us decide our future through conventional use.

Chapter 3 Principles of Social Media

Social media rules are conventions for comfortable contact with contacts. Guidelines are things to consider. Some include a range of activity. Others explain what may be comfortable or uncomfortable. Quality relationships are what we strive for through engagement.

Social Media Rules

- Engage others without hate because it is extreme and unreasonable.
- Share genuine content with contacts because it shows you care about the relationship.
- Refrain from cursing or swearing because it is cyberbullying.
- Show regard for the wishes of others when posting because respect is a quality of friendship.
- Share accurate information, check facts, because errors invalidate communication.

- Correct small mistakes and delete misinformation because it adds value to the network.
- Refrain from using offensive usernames because it is extreme to be recognized as offensive.
- Don't share the personal information of others without permission because it breaches privacy.
- Do everything in moderation because it promotes good content. Moderate content.

Guidelines

Time

Social Media is used daily by some sporadically by others. Setting time boundaries controls the process. It is done within a controlled time period. Budgeting and planning allow examination of actions for improvement. They prevent overuse.

Usernames

Friends cannot follow you if they do not know how to find you. To make a name for ourselves on the internet we have to keep it across networks and domains. Variations are common when exact matches are not available. This builds personal brands with an identifying mark.

Writing

Writers compose documents with correct grammar in paragraphs. Writing for layout purposes encourages people to read it. Short paragraphs are preferred by readers. Two sentence paragraphs are acceptable. Brief grammatical composition of complete thoughts is well liked.

Emoticons

Emoticons convey feelings through text : D They replace periods. Use them to add meaning to posts. It sets the tone.

Reading

Users post and send text. It must be read. Reply or comment after the entire message has been consumed. You may get the wrong message if you do not read an entire post.

Shares

People share content created by others. One share for every ten is common. Filtering content and focusing on engaging contacts is a strategy to increase popularity where it applies. Give shares to get shared.

Employers

The things written in status updates may help or hurt chances of getting jobs, promotions, or keeping them. Follow company culture because we are representative of the companies we work for.

Human resources departments monitor social media. Profiles of prospective and current employees are engaged.

Statements

Absolute statements invite negative comments because they do not leave room for exceptions. Precise open ended statements encourage positive engagement.

An absolute statement can often be negated by example. Specific open ended statements leave room for exceptions and alternatives. They are true in a specific instance.

Filters

Filters distort pictures. Adding them can turn a picture that is not so great into a great one. They change color, tones, and pixelate pictures in an artistic way. The content is changed to add more value to contacts.

Credibility

Credible sources have a good record for publishing accurate information, stories, and blogs. Cite them because truthful sources contribute to high quality content. Information on the internet is not trustworthy unless it is credible. Credibility comes from credible contacts.

News

Breaking news starts as a blog. Articles are often written after a story develops. Sharing news helps stories develop. Blogs are personal opinions related to topics of interest. Sharing good blogs develops good news.

Following

Following an account is a public association. A direct connection to their content. Followers are listed in profiles. They receive updates in their content feeds. Direct communication is sometimes possible.

For followers, we have to follow first. There is no set number of how many to follow for others to follow. Following must be genuine and include re-posting material.

Following others without expectation of following in return is genuine. Those who like the content created and curated will follow. They have shared interests.

Influencers have a large following and a lot of friends. They set trends with content they share related to the interests of their friends and followers. Follow influencers for leadership.

Cross-Posting

Cross-posting is the practice of posting the same content to multiple networks. Use unique descriptions with keywords tailored to each network. Search Engine Optimization (SEO) is different by domain. Keywords relevant to the domain help. Data is available for different domains (See Appendix A for keyword research websites).

Influencers

Influencers become popular by joining groups, following others, and curating content. Friending and following influencers provides access to their network and content. This is method of becoming influential by engaging a large audience of interested followers.

Hashtag

A hashtag (#) is the pound sign on a number pad. Placing it at the beginning of a word includes it in a topical search for many social sites. It turns them into links that can be searched by clicking.

Using popular hashtags is an effective optimization technique. Performing keyword research for them works even better. Keywords may be hashtags themselves or associated with popular topics (See Appendix A for keyword research websites).

Social Media

Pictures, blogs, social networks, reading networks, and audio networks are categories of popular social domains. Social Media is the interactive dissemination of information through the internet, User Generated Content (UGC), between contacts.

Social websites provide news based on personal relationships with content from contacts. Contacts are friends. Content can be created, shared, and changed. We control the content of the network.

Friends are people we engage. Social means friends. It is a personal relationship. These relationships are cultivated through the types of social media.

Share

People share and reshare content they create and content created by others. We create content by posting. Others share it by posting it to their network.

The number of times others repost content is publicly tracked on many networks. This is a quality measurement.

Like

There are buttons that provide public affirmation of content without commenting. They are generally considered 'like' buttons. Many are heart shaped.

Associated clicks represent affirmation of the content or page. The number of people who affirm it is tracked. This is a quality measurement.

Comments

A comment is a written opinion about a post. We may post comments on content. They are public.

The text appears below the content. They ordered by date. Comments are posted less frequently than other affirmation. This is a quality measurement.

Pictures

A picture is an image that can be taken by a camera or drawn by various methods. Graphic images represent people, places, and things that can be seen.

They are the most engaging content across all networks that allow them. Some networks have them as a theme. A computer picture, graphic, is an image in a digital format. These include JPEG ".jpg" and PNG ".png".

Smiles are positive and have a positive effect on viewers. They are contagious. Some of us make and accept friend requests based on profile pictures. We post candid, professional, and semi-professional pictures often.

Blogs

Blogs are personal and organizational. The word is the combination of web and log. The web is the internet. A log is a record of opinions.

The content is generated to log opinions. A post is a form of one to many communications. One person posts information. Many people read it.

Logs, posts, track changes. Posts are not absolute. A blog is an internet log of opinions about a topic or theme. They change over time.

Nothing is absolute. We can make up our own minds and change them. How we feel is our own decision.

Microblogs

A Microblog allows connections to share opinions within brief character limits. We can follow or subscribe to the posts of others. Others can follow our posts.

A fact is something most people agree upon. Research determines fact. Microblog posts are opinions that may contain facts.

The character limit does not permit complex statements because they usually involve two or more ideas. It is hard to fit two or more ideas into one microblog post because it would take up too many characters.

Social Networks

A Social Network is a domain that allows people to connect with contacts to share information about common interests through various media.

Contacts have permission to communicate within defined levels of access. Connections make it a network. Contact makes it social. Networks must be engaged.

They allow one to one, one to many, and many to many communications. These methods are contact classes. They are further divided by features, preferences, and access.

Reading

Books and short stories have social networks. Literary works are the theme of engagement. Sharing from readers and authors creates the content.

A literary work is a set of text arranged so it can be read in order. The writing is published. People read about topics and issues. Then they engage.

A bookshelf is a common feature. This is a list of works read. Clicking the work provides further information about it.

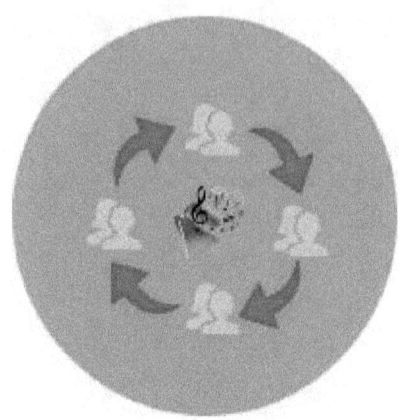

Audio

Audio has social networks with music and podcasts as the theme. Contacts listen and share audio through them. Music is the arrangement of sounds that are pleasant to those that can hear them. A podcast is a topical voice recording.

Quality

A contact stored in a list created from engagement is a friend. It requires relational database association. Profile and content views are the lowest measurable level.

Engagement determines quality. It is a subjective term that can be measured by objective standards.

Contacts read and comment on quality content. They engage updates with comments, replies, likes, re-posts, and shares. These are the measurable standards that require contact.

Social Currency

Social currency is influential content. Engaging posts shared with your network have influence. An engagement strategy provides contacts with social currency.

Article links, tips, and news about current trends have a high social value. Influencers share high quality social currency. Find, create, and share this content with contacts. Research can be done to find influencers and influential content (See Appendix A for a list of websites).

Strategy

An engagement strategy is a Social Media Optimization marketing term that describes the most basic strategy. It treats all contacts the same. The way it is described here is not marketing because testing is not done. The techniques are the same.

Posting social currency three times a day during different time periods from an account increases engagement. In practice posting three times a month is acceptable.

Finding influential content to share, resharing influencers, and using keywords and hashtags is the most important part of the strategy. Research is necessary. The same keywords and hashtags can be reused. Alternatively, new research can be done for each post.

Managing online profiles requires monitoring, contribution, and measurement. 'Lurk before you leap'. Contribute social currency. See how much people like it. There are free and freemium products that automate the process

(See Chapter 7 and Appendix A for a website list).

Timing

There are 24 hours in a day. Days have four general time periods, morning, afternoon, evening, and night. They can be divide into six hour increments.

Posting during each time period is acceptable. Three or four posts a day from a given account is optimal. The exact time can be determined by analytics. Most people sleep at night. This time period is generally not included.

Chapter 4 Principles of Mobile

Mobile rules are common beliefs, principles. Guidelines are basic truths without any specifics because device manufacturers provide varying features and benefits. Comfortable communication is the goal. This includes transactions in the Information Age.

Mobile Rules

- Watch out to prevent accidents because distraction has to be mitigated.
- Consume data appropriate for everyone around because screens are public.
- Be present in reality while engaged because it is easy to get detached.
- Don't download big files or stream during peak hotspot times because it slows down the network.
- Think about use beforehand because it makes it more productive.
- Check the signal strength before you stream because you can't stream with a low signal.

- Know establishment rules before using a hotspot to avoid breaking them.
- Know the features of devices and apps used regularly because it saves time.
- Follow the cultural norms of the crowd around you because humanity comes first.
- Accept that online activities are monitored in public hotspots because user agreements allow it.

Guidelines

Memory

Low memory prevents downloads, use, and can slow down all operations of a device. Clear app cache memory from the device settings app menu. Clear browsing data from the browser (privacy) settings menu. Uninstall apps from the device settings app menu.

Upload pictures to social networks or other cloud storage (See Appendix A for a list). Then delete them on the device. All this can be done so devices operate optimally because data storage is limited and affects device performance.

Battery

Battery energy can be conserved to make it last longer. Location tracking drains the battery. Turn it off until needed by an app to save energy.

Automatic updates use battery energy that can be saved. Turn off automatic updates. Update apps when the device is plugged in to prevent unnecessary battery drain.

Camera

Smart devices have cameras. The Rule of Thirds applies for taking off center pictures (see chapter 9 for guidelines). Cropping according to it catches the eye.

Light blue is a good color for taking pictures. It brings out flesh tones and compliments almost any background. Bright pictures are the most well liked. Light and filters make pictures bright.

Mobile

Mobile is a classification of products and services that exchange information through wireless communication. Wireless data is a service provided by carriers. Easily movable electronics are mobile.

Devices include smartphones, tablets, laptops, wearables, and automobiles. The Operating System (OS) makes these 'things', mobile devices, smart. Wireless connectivity allows the OS to exchange data through the internet.

Self-Monitoring Analysis and Reporting Technology (SMART) applications define the class of products. They may be downloaded and installed from app stores. Electronics with Android, iOS, and Windows Phone are mobile.

Apps provide a new level of organization and assistance for our activities and relationships. They are transforming society as a whole. The way we are operating systematically changes with optimization provided by apps.

Operating System

OS's control a device. Apps tell it what to do. Telephone, internet, cameras, location, audio, touchscreen, input keys, and Bluetooth are the hardware whose functions are controlled by apps.

The set of controls allows apps to use them. They can be downloaded from an app store. Alphabet's Android and Apple's Internet Operating System (iOS) are the most popular. Windows Phone is notable for smartphones.

Android

Android is controlled by Alphabet through the Open Handset Alliance. The OS covers devices, wearables, and automobiles. Source code is based on Linux open source code. It is the most popular because it is installed on the most devices.

Versions have a number and a name. It was founded in 2003 by a group of developers. Devices range from low end entry level models to high end premium products.

Alphabet, named Google at the time, bought it in 2005. The Open Handset Alliance was created in 2007 to set standards for the code. Version 1.0 was released in 2008.

Apps for Android mobile can be downloaded from the Google Play Store and various other app stores. Alphabet sets its own standards. They review apps before they are placed in the store.

iOS

The iPhone was introduced in 2007 with iOS. The iPhone, iPod, iPad, Apple Watch, and Apple TV use it. CarPlay is an app for automobiles that uses it.

Versions are numbered. The iTunes App Store launched in 2008. It is the exclusive distributor of apps for iOS.

Apple manufactures premium products. They are generally more expensive than comparable competitors. Steve Jobs is credited with the company's development.

Windows Phone

Windows Phone is a mobile OS developed by Microsoft that launched in 2010. Windows Phone 7 was the first Windows Phone OS. Apps can be downloaded from the Windows Phone Store.

Microsoft acquired Nokia, a mobile handset and tablet manufacturer, in 2013. This acquisition has allowed Microsoft to partner with websites and software developers for new products and services.

Feature Phone

Technically, a cell phone with a web browser is a smartphone because websites are applications. Visiting a site allows use of the app. Preinstalled apps allow smart use.

A feature phone is a cellular telephone that connects to a wireless carrier for voice and data services. The services provided are preinstalled prior to sale. They are controlled and updated by the wireless carrier.

Email, contact managers, calendars, and web browsers are common preinstalled apps. These services are what made the first smartphone.

Wearable

A wearable is an electronic device controlled by a mobile OS with downloadable apps. They are generally synchronized with other devices. Android and iOS have wearables.

Smart watches, glasses, and clothes are wearables. Android Wear and Apple Watch have multiple downloadable apps in app stores designed specifically for the devices.

Activity trackers, clothes, and glasses are available. Apps are designed by manufacturers for iOS and Android that synchronize information from these wearables.

Automobile

Android Auto and iOS CarPlay are apps for automobiles. The stereo must be compatible with the app. Many car manufacturers provide compatibility with new models. New stereos can be installed with the apps.

The display is an infotainment center for automobiles. Regular stereo capabilities are available. The display also synchronizes with smartphones. This makes the apps available on a smartphone available for display in the car. Some car functions may be controlled through the app.

Apps

Apps provide instructions to the OS for use. Developers program them. Hardware is controlled by software.

Cameras have apps that take pictures, capture video, and scan barcodes. Websites have browser apps for navigation. The sites are applications themselves as well. Maps use location services as standalone apps and features of others. These are a few examples.

Type

Utility, productivity, and entertainment are the types. All software fits into these categories. App stores have many overlapping subcategories to sell them (See Appendix B for a list).

Utility apps are software applications that use the device itself. File managers and communication. Productivity apps allow file creation. Word processing and spreadsheets. Entertainment apps enable audio and video. Media players and games.

Utility is the reason the mobile industry was created. Mobile phones provide the utility of communication. The internet is a utility. All transmission is communication.

Entertainment apps in the subcategory of social networking and games are the most popular. Social networking apps allow one to many communication, updates and posts. Game apps engage us to manipulate data for a desired outcome, goal completion.

App Stores

App stores distribute apps. Each OS has an official store where apps can be downloaded.

Google Play is the official store for Android with all their apps. Others are allowed to distribute them as well. The iTunes App Store is the exclusive distributor for iOS. Links to app stores are provided on developer and other websites.

Sales are driven by advertising. Feedback plays an important role. There are three business models for distribution, free, freemium, and premium.

Feedback

Feedback includes customer reviews and star ratings. App star ratings are based on customer satisfaction. They are displayed in different ways depending on the store.

People often leave feedback when they have a bad experience. It takes a lot of successful downloads to receive positive feedback. Purchasing an app without feedback is taking a risk with data and device because they collect data and have been known to contain malware.

Free

Free means without cost. Apps are given away without costs for a variety of reasons. Often revenue is earned through advertising on free apps. Branding and exposure are a compelling reason to give an app away.

Freemium

Freemium is the combination of free and premium. Free apps with premium features. The business model is used to generate In App Purchases (IAP). Apps offer added functionality and versions without advertising as premium features and benefits. Video games charge users for virtual goods that enhance the game.

An IAP is the payment for a good or service within the app being used. The revenue generated from IAP is higher on a Cost Per Install (CPI) basis because there are more installations. Stores give their apps away.

Successful companies have switched to the freemium model in whole or in part because consumers will not pay. Instead they use the free versions of competing apps sacrificing features and benefits or screen space to advertising.

Microsoft Office productivity apps are an example. They were premium apps. Now they are free to use online with limited features. Premium versions may be purchased for use online and download and installation.

Premium

Premium apps cost money to download and install. Price points vary. Those that perform a specific function relative to us and device cost more. Those with alternatives cost less.

Mobile Website

A website is an app that uses a browser app for viewing. Software types, utility, productivity, and entertainment, apply.

Browsers are preinstalled and available in app stores.

Optimized sites look the same as apps in stores. The programming is the same for modern apps. Some websites redirect mobile users to completely different sites.

Alternatively, browsers scale sites that are not optimized and allow zooming. Scrolling may be used without optimization or scaling.

Smartphone

The first smartphone was the Sidekick I released in 2002. It had Internet access, preinstalled apps, and a cloud storage data plan. The company that created it, Danger, was founded by former Apple employees.

A smartphone is a cellular telephone with a mobile OS. It allows us to install apps. They can be downloaded from app stores.

More powerful versions of feature phone apps are preinstalled on smartphones. Larger screens, better processors, and more features makes use more comfortable. Alternatives to preinstalled apps with more or less of the same features can be found in app stores.

Tablet

A tablet is an open face touch screen computer that can be held in your hands. A handheld computer with a mobile OS. Smartphone apps work on a tablets with the same operating system.

Some apps are designed specifically for them. Others are optimized to adjust to the size of the screen. Standard sizes range from 7 to 12 inches.

Keyboards and cases are popular upgrades and accessories. Laptop computers are sometimes given touchscreens to make them a laptop and tablet, 2 in 1. Smartphones are given large screens to make them smartphones and tablets, phablets.

Phablet

A phablet is a smartphone with a large screen and stylus. The word is the combination of phone and tablet. They range in size from 5.5 to 6.5 inches.

Their size allows more comfortable use for a lot of apps. A stylus is a modern computing instrument with a small rod and rubber tip for input on touch screens. These make use more productive.

Laptop

A laptop is a computer with a full size keyboard attached to a monitor. OS's are designed for the increased processing power larger devices have. Windows, Mac, Chrome, and Linux are the most popular.

These devices are easily movable. They have batteries, are designed to close for carrying, and have wireless internet connections.

Almost every type of app is available to Windows devices because they can emulate other OS's. Mac OS is preferred by programmers. Chrome is user friendly.

Connectivity

Mobile connectivity is the condition of connection. It is required for mobile communication, the internet. Data travels between electronics in air waves.

Microwaves make it possible. They were introduced into telecommunications in 1950. Governments regulate the spectrum used to transmit data through air waves.

Hotspot

A Hotspot provides short range device connectivity, internet access. They use microwaves for broadband connections.

A wireless local Area Network (WLAN) connects to an Internet Service Provider (ISP) through a router to make a hotspot. Connectivity is affected by the number of users and amount of bandwidth they are using.

Businesses offer hotspots to attract patrons. Many homes have them. Mobile hotspots are available for personal use.

Wireless Carrier

A wireless carrier is a Mobile Network Operator (MNO). They own, rent, or control the radio frequency spectrum that their products and services use. This distinguishes them from resellers of their services.

MNO's control cellular towers. The more towers an MNO has the better the connectivity. They allow more connections and less disconnection due to capacity.

Communication

Our mobile devices are always on providing the opportunity to communicate through the internet. Being present in the moment instead of online is an expectation based on relationship status with those around us. Social constraints require transparency for comfortable use.

Let people know if you have to use a mobile device. In social settings, it can be annoying to those ignored in order to avoid a topic of discussion. Speakers often encourage live microblogging. Event hashtags are promoted for use.

It depends on the people you are around. Sharing information about them requires permission. Tolerance should be given to those who do go off into cyberspace.

Shopping

A mobile shopper is a person who uses a mobile device to research goods and services as well as make purchases. A mobile buyer is a mobile shopper, but a mobile shopper is not necessarily a mobile buyer. Shoppers do not always buy. Buyers always shop.

Economies are transaction based. So, making everyone comfortable with ecommerce (m-commerce) is the goal of informatization. This movement led government and business is to make information the basis of our economy. This means the internet.

Ecommerce is m-commerce. It allows users to purchase products or services with an online checkout. App stores and apps that allow IAP provide m-commerce.

Android Pay, Apple Pay, and Samsung Pay are popular payment apps accepted by retailers. Point of Sale (POS) systems accept their payment. Payments are IAP.

Chapter 5 Principles of Online Education

Education rules prescribe ways to interact with learners. Guidelines outline activities required for full participation. Explanations of the process provide insight for success. Continuous education is a component of the Information Age.

Education Rules

- Teach and promote peace because violence has to be taught to use.
- Follow the rules. Don't use copyrighted material without permission because it is against the rules.
- Argue issues, topics, and subjects not prejudices or irrelevant points because attacks are bullying.
- Follow the teacher. Stay on topic because changing the subject distracts learners.
- Refrain from sharing personal information because the internet is insecure.

- Balance online learning because it is easier to remember what is learned with diverse activities.
- Show kindness to classmates because it makes it easier to learn. Good relationships help the class.
- Help others and they will help you because the class benefits from the success of members.
- Data is not real it is a learning tool. Be present in reality because we learn to be part of society.

Guidelines

System Requirements

System requirements are the minimum hardware and software required to participate in an online course. Operating System, software, and browsers need to be checked for compatibility. Recommended software should be installed. It may have its own requirements.

For Windows machines it is common to change the path of environment variables when computer programming applications are installed. It can take hours or days to install the prerequisite software for participation in a class.

Course material may be designed for a certain browser and version. General education assignments require certain document formats. Accounts may be required to use free software. Download and installation of free productivity software is an alternative (See Appendix A for a list).

Searching for Answers

Search engines provide the answers to many questions. Most are capable of computation. Queries return relevant results for actual assignment questions. There are many online tutorials that can be found to answer questions in class modules.

Forum Help

Class discussion forums generally contain the answers to all questions a student may have. When they do not, ask. Searching for the answer prior to asking is required.

Questions that already have answers may not get a response. In some cases, the answer includes a link to a previous answer. Posting links to helpful tutorials is often done. Post and follow.

Education

Online Education is acquired knowledge taught through the internet. Scholarship is an underlying belief. Learning from study is the process measured by achievement. Self-study is a major part of it.

Protocol has been developed for the organized teaching and measuring of the acquisition of knowledge. Schools are organizations for education with their own protocol. Social acceptance of computers in school occurred after Time Magazine named the computer 'Man of The Year' in 1982.

School

Schools are organizations that bring us together to share knowledge. They provide certificates as a base measure of scholarship. We are measured by feedback from assignments and answers on exams.

Knowledge is factual information and skill acquired from study. Facts are remembered. Skill is developed from the application of information.

Scholarship is the experience of learning measured by achievement. Experiences may be coursework, articles, or anything else online that teaches skills. The measure is the application of skills acquired from experiences. It is denoted by good practice, work.

Learning

Learning is a process for the acquisition of knowledge. Audio, video, and text are consumed in online methods. Projects are completed. Discussion forums provide answers to questions.

There is free online education in principle because learning is the acquisition of knowledge. Most knowledge can be found on the internet. It can be acquired.

In practice, there are websites that charge money for certificates and education. They are not well regarded. Some are better than others.

Study

Study is any activity in the learning process. Texts include eBooks, articles, presentation slides, and discussion forums. EBook formats are ePub, mobi, Portable Document Format (PDF), and website. A textbook is simply the text used to acquire knowledge. Physical textbooks can be used.

Videotaped slide show presentations may serve as the only information provided by professors for an online class. Discussion forums answer the questions we have. Presentation slides are available for viewing and download.

Online learning is self-study. It is the acquisition of knowledge without direct supervision. There is no classroom. Teachers do not directly supervise learning.

Achievement

Certificates are provided by schools for classes to measure scholarship. This marks the beginning. Portfolios, practice, and application prove knowledge has been acquired.

The use of computers in education has made taking classes a matter of routine rather than scholarship. There is no question that electronics make us smart. Skills must be applied to claim ability.

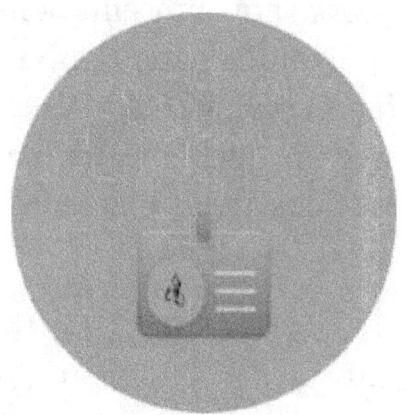

Student

A student is a member of a class studying in a school. Schools organize classes for students. Participants, students, study to learn. They are educated.

Class

A class is merely a group. An online class is a correspondence course. They are collections of knowledge about a subject or topic arranged to explain information to participants for professional use or personal interest.

Participants are students. The group is an order. They follow the instructions of their teachers in order. Weeks are segmented by modules that determine the order of skill acquisition.

Tutorial

Tutorials are training. They teach specific skills. Classes teach multiple skills.

Social Media contains a lot of tutorials. Blogs and videos teach many popular skills. There are free blogs and other domains that provide them exclusively (See Appendix A). Many do not require registration.

College

A college is a self-governing society for instruction and study. It is higher education after primary, middle, and secondary school. The word was originally used to describe construction schools where Masons went to learn their trade.

There are some religious implications. Masons take actions for God. They built many historic

Churches. The Catholic College of Cardinals determines the Pope (religious leader).

MOOC

MOOC is an acronym for Massive Open Online Course (MOOC). Massive describes the scale. Hundreds of thousands of people may be in one class. Open enrollment allows anyone to sign up. There are fees for most classes.

Peer and automated grading is used for feedback on assignments. Teachers assistants monitor discussion forums providing answers to questions. Course lectures are recycled for new terms.

Continuing Education

Continuing education is the knowledge acquired after compulsory education has been completed. Traditionally, it has been a professional requirement for association members to maintain their status.

This type of learning is done with short part time courses. The description fits some online classes and most tutorials. Availability and use has made them crucial for acquiring new skills and career advancement.

The cost of education is significantly lowered when delivered through the internet. This removes barriers that previously kept poor, minorities, and women from learning skills. It is not easy to learn online, but it is achievable.

We must continue our education compelled by inspiration and aspiration because technology is evolving rapidly. The resources exist online. We must learn to be part of the Information Age.

Chapter 6 Principles of Internet Safety

Safety rules are the most important techniques we can follow because they make us feel comfortable in general. The guidelines provide solutions to known problems that the technology industry believes will help. Awareness provides protection because proper precautions cannot be taken without it. It requires a new way of thinking.

Safety Rules

- Print and save receipts with a product description because they are proof of purchase for disputes.
- Use an uppercase letter, number, and character for a strong password because they are hard to crack.
- Don't share personal information with unknown contacts because fake profiles are common.
- Use antivirus software because computers are under constant attack.
- Keep your password private because sharing it compromises the network.

- Backup important files because data can easily be lost by accident, virus, or hack.

- Update software regularly because out of date programs are vulnerable to attack.

- Read privacy policies because information collection and sharing practices are explained in them.

- Online friends are not real friends because we don't meet with them. Cyber friends share and like.

Guidelines

Two Factor Authentication
Two Factor Authentication (TFA or 2FA) is a login process that requires two steps. Each

step is a factor. It should be used to protect accounts where available.

An email address and password are one factor. A time sensitive code is sent as the second factor. It can be sent to by email, Short Message Service (SMS), or app.

Photo Tagging

Photos can be tagged with name and location in social media. Once enough photos are tagged, facial recognition software can recognize that name and face anywhere. Social networks use the software.

It takes is four pictures to be identified by facial recognition software anywhere. A face in the background of a photo can be recognized. We can be identified in group photos.

Granting permission to take pictures is a privacy concern with safety implications. Signing a release to attend festivals and concerts becomes a factor in determining whether or not to attend. Posting pictures of others is something to think about.

Password Recovery

Password recovery is a backup method for accessing an account once the password has been lost, hacked, or account locked. Recovery email addresses and phone numbers are used for authentication to regain access.

These options can be found in security or other settings. Look for them. Provide the necessary information. This option has to be enabled separate from TFA.

Connections

Data transfer requires open connections to send and receive. Wire, cable, wireless, Bluetooth, and infrared are types. Protection from intrusion can be done by closing connections.

Disconnecting from the internet and closing connections when not in use is safe. Turn off WiFi and Bluetooth when not in use on mobile devices. Discoverability is a Bluetooth setting that should be off unless devices are being paired. Infrared accessories may be disconnected.

Privacy

Privacy is being undisturbed by others from observation or intrusion. The best way to stay safe on the internet is to limit your exposure. Keep information from the observation or intrusion of others.

'Arm's length' is often used to describe privacy protection. Anything beyond the reach of our arms is too far away for personal contact. Account settings have controls that limit exposure for privacy reasons.

Privacy settings hide information. Public view is the most exposure. Private is limited view by user class. Block excludes accounts from viewing. Social media, mobile devices, and web browsers have privacy settings.

Safety

Internet Safety is freedom from harm, potential danger, and victimization by criminals on the internet. This is an underlying belief of users. We believe in safe communication.

It is built on knowledge of computer security and personal safety. Computer security is data protection and maintenance. Personal safety is physical and electronic.

Personal

Protection from unauthorized or harmful access to computer data through network connections is the primary purpose of internet security. We have personal data on our computers. Viruses are unauthorized and harmful access. There are various methods of data protection for freedom from viruses or other security.

Computers and websites are not sufficiently protected from unwanted access for many reasons. Harmful software programs and websites can be designed to collect the same information collected by helpful software and websites.

Hoax

A hoax is a fraud. Trickery and treachery are included. A systematic plan to steal money is usually involved. It is a scam. Not always, but most of the time. They are online tricks for fun or scam.

Phishing

Phishing is a hoax to trick people into sharing sensitive information in a variety of ways. Identities are stolen. Computer data is compromised.

Fake websites and bogus emails ask users to reveal pin and passwords while posing as banks or other institutions. Targeted emails are sent requesting that recipients follow links.

Once the link is followed computers may be hacked through security flaws. Personal information may be requested.

Fake mobile banking websites trick people into revealing their usernames and passwords. The small screens make it difficult to tell the difference between real and fake.

Rich Friend

A popular scam begins by telling the victim they have a rich friend. A person sends an email with an elaborate story about riches they or a friend have. They need your help to get them. Sometimes a fake check is sent to the victim who cashes it and sends non-negotiable funds to the scammer.

The check received is negotiable. When it does not clear the person who cashed it owes the money. The person who received the bulk of the cash is generally out of the reach of local authorities.

Antivirus

Antivirus prevents unwanted access to computer data. It blocks access. A program scans for known viruses. Once found it deletes and quarantines them.

Types include desktop, mobile, and internet. Good desktop versions include router protection as well. Mobile cleanup apps are a form.

Some are sold through the freemium and subscription business model. Programs are continuously updated with virus definitions. It is a service.

Browsers have popup blockers and anti-phishing features. They can be turned on and off because it limits access to sites. They are turned on by default.

Virus

A virus is software installed without knowledge or consent. It is capable of copying itself to other programs and computers for harmful purposes. Malware, Spyware, Ransomware, and Scareware are types.

Malware alters data once installed. It deletes files or otherwise corrupts them. All data is typically lost.

Spyware collects information. It transmits the data to another computer. Keystroke identifiers are a form used to steal passwords and credit card numbers.

Ransomware locks users out of a program or computer until money is paid to remove it. Access is denied until the hacker is paid.

Scareware uses popup messages to have a virus removed. Browsers can be infected. Popup messages offer antivirus software to remove the virus popup for a price.

Computer Maintenance

Computer maintenance is the preservation of components for operation. Electronics may be unsafe if not properly maintained. Clean, unbroken, and protected are maintenance techniques for devices.

Devices should be cleaned regularly. How they are cleaned is a matter of style. There are a variety of products and methods for cleaning screens and keyboards.

Cracked screens and frayed wires should be replaced. Repair shops carry screens. New cables and wires can be found at electronics stores. Cases are available for carrying electronics.

Mobile

Mobile safety is a serious issue. Mobile electronics have more safety issues than stationary devices because they are used in more situations. There are more chances to hack a mobile device because it passes through networks when carried. Distraction from device use is a major concern.

There are a wide range of apps that may mitigate some issues. Use is highly situational. Antivirus is necessary. Beyond that it becomes a tradeoff that balances security, memory, and type of use.

Safe Thinking

The Internet is becoming the basis of society led by government and business. Thinking of the things we do online in the same sense we do them in reality is safe thinking. Our computers serve as physical infrastructure.

Purchasing items online makes the computer a store and wallet. Online banking makes it a bank. Social media makes it our friend.

We have to treat our devices as such. Wallets are secured by us. Banks have a lot of security.

Friends keep things private from groups. It is a safe way of thinking about internet use.

Chapter 7 Principles of Online Business

Business rules apply to consumers. All we have to do is accept it. Guidelines can be followed by all of us for transactions and social media. Explanations of the fundamental propositions helps. Measurable formulas provide a basis for action.

Business Rules

- Record transactions. Make sure you get a receipt or provide one because it is a record.
- Use a professional signature with a name, number, and company because it validates messages.
- Ask for clarification before you act because once something is done wrong it may be hard to fix.
- Refrain from writing in text because slang is unclear and ambiguous.
- Double space paragraphs because white space makes text more readable.
- Use descriptive headings because it gives writing context.

- Reference business reasons because immediate clarification may be difficult.

Guidelines

Transparency

Transparency in business is motivation and practices that are easy to perceive. We prefer to do business with people and entities that we know and understand. A layer of accountability is added when we understand what is being done for or to us. We know if it is being done right.

Management Decision Science

We are able to determine online activity with certainty because digital data is discrete. It can be counted individually. Activity that increases business can be measured by a Key

Performance Indicator (KPI). Identifying them for use in decision making is management.

Management Decision Science (MDS) uses quantitative data for statistical analysis to make business decisions. Finance, accounting, and marketing decisions are made this way. Data is collected for applying formulas that report costs, generate ratios, and measure demand. They determine a proper course of business action.

Social Media Manager

Social Media Manager is a job function in business similar to accounting. The position is to monitor, contribute, and measure social media accounts. Accounting formulas are the basis of Social Media Management Systems (SMMS).

SMMS have software (See Appendix A for a list), strategies, and techniques for creating content. These functions are necessary because the internet is becoming the basis of our economy. Social media is a customer service function in business because customers use it.

Email Marketing

Newsletters are email marketing. A tool used to engage high value markets. The most likely customers to purchase a product or service subscribe to these lists.

Messages periodically sent to subscribers are newsletters. Monthly is standard. Best practices for newsletters depend on the market.

Weekly messages are sent by electronic retail (etail) companies. Monthly and quarterly editions are sent by organizations. Bi-weekly and daily newsletters are sent by news organizations.

A/B Testing

A/B Testing compares variables with defined outcomes to see which has the highest number. Every section of a webpage document can be tested. Social media content is tested. Email campaigns do it.

Different versions of content are shown to viewers. Conversion rates are measured. The content with the highest conversion wins. There is no way to know if content is optimal without testing. Everything should be tested.

Returns

Items purchased online can be returned through the mail or to the brick and mortar store depending on the retailer. There is a different address from the shipping address for returns. Do not mail returns to the shipping address. Most online retailers require authorization before an item can be returned.

Obtain permission and the proper return mailing address before attempting to send an item back to an online retailer. Call the customer service phone number for the return address and authorization.

Disputes

If there is a dispute about an item contact the retailer first. Disputes can arise if you do not receive an item, the item is delivered in damaged condition, or it is not as described. These are common reasons for disputes.

If you are not satisfied with the resolution provided by the retailer contact the financial institution used to make payment. Call your bank. Banks and credit card issuers have their own dispute process that is customer centric. Follow the instructions and provide them with a copy of the product description and payment confirmation for the best outcome.

Business

We all know what business is, but it may not be that easy to define because there is so much involved. Business is transactional. There are a lot of layers before and after a transaction. A transaction is in the middle.

Online Business is the exchange of goods and services assisted by the internet. There are three categories, Business to Consumer (B2C), Consumer to Consumer (C2C), and Business to Business (B2B).

Hyperlocal

Hyperlocal describes community centric business. The term is often used to describe local ecommerce. Community based products and services. Grocery delivery is hyperlocal because they are delivered locally from within the community.

Professional Social Networks

A Professional Social Network is a domain that allows us to connect with contacts to share information about how we earn a living through various media. It is a social media social network with earning a living as the primary focus.

Ecommerce

Ecommerce is online shopping, banking, and bill pay. The purchase of goods and services online. This includes buying apps as well as retail merchandise from online stores.

Payment Options

Online payment options include credit or debit cards, online banks, and ACH (electronic checks). Credit cards are the safest method for processing online transactions because they do not affect your cash balance if they are fraudulently used.

PayPal is an online payment method similar to a debit card. It's a checking account whose primary focus is online transactions. For many people PayPal serves as a buffer between the checking account they use for daily activity and one they use for online transactions.

Online Banking

Online banking is logging into an online account with direct access to funds in that account. It benefits us because we do not have to go into bank branch offices to perform financial transactions.

It allows us to perform banking activity during non-banking hours. Online banking is secure. Banks use secure connections, encrypted data transfer, and high programming standards to protect assets.

Online Bill Pay

Paying bills online is a convenient way to perform a routine task. It is as safe as the website used and connection used to access it. Safety and security depends on the providers.

Save a copy of the payment confirmation page and backup the saved copy for record keeping.

A lot of companies encourage us to go paperless when we pay bills online. They want us to receive statements via email. If paper bills are preferred look for a checkbox with that option. Alternatively, we can call the company to make a request.

Classifieds

Classifieds are advertisements for employment or to sell items arranged by category published by a domain. Domains facilitate transactions. Employers and sellers post. Job seekers and buyers respond.

Auction

A standard auction is a sales process in which potential buyers bid on an item in a contest to be the highest. The time period is set at the beginning. Domains manage the process and collect payment.

Marketing

Advertising is the placement of marketing messages online for delivery to consumers. The messages are designed to get consumers to purchase a product or service. It attracts public attention for a business to sell products and services with paid announcements.

This involves offering deals, discounts, contests, and special content to consumers. Deals and discounts can be offered with promotion codes.

Search Engine Optimization

Search Engine Optimization (SEO) is the process of making content appear higher in

Search Engine Results Pages (SERP's). There are two types of SEO, white and black hat. White hat SEO is ethical. Black hat SEO employs unethical techniques.

Search engines rank content by keywords, tags, and backlinks. Search bots looks for keywords and tags. The engine processes how many backlinks there are to a URL. The rank and reputation of sites linking in is evaluated to determine the pagerank for a given search.

Optimization uses keywords to find an audience for content. It involves keyword placement in content for higher rankings on SERP's. A keyword is a word that indicates the meaning of a passage. They are used by information retrieval systems, search engines, to find relevant content.

Research involves finding highly ranked keywords and synonyms to use in content and descriptions (See Appendix A for a list of websites). This makes the content available to an interested audience. In theory, good content ranks highest because viewers engage it to raise the ranking. In practice businesses pay for SEO and advertising to raise the rank of content.

Planning reveals opportunities for content to be viewed. Changing the keywords in content from those with high competition to low competition could increase views because there is more opportunity for optimized content to appear high on SERP's. Having a high ranking will generally garner more hits than a low one.

Tags

Search engines look for tags to give content meaning. They are semantic. Pictures, links, and web pages all have separate HTML tags or attributes that search engines look for. Semantic search engines look for RDF tags.

Pictures and links have descriptive elements that can be included in HTML tags to help give them meaning. Pictures use alt tags. Links use title tags. Websites use Metadata.

All pictures should have alt tags within the image tag. Links should have title tags contained within the anchor tag. Keyword and description meta tags are necessary in the header (See Appendix C for sample code).

RDF tags are used to describe semantic entities. It is a syntax for describing things. Open Graph is a popular format for writing RDF tags. Popular search engines sponsor schema.org structured data, which includes RDFa tags.

Backlinks

A backlink is an incoming hyperlink from one web page to another. They are the largest contributor to a web pages SERP ranking. The quality of the site that has the link to another is figured into the equation that determines SERP's.

Social Media Optimization

Social Media Optimization (SMO) is a term that describes techniques used to increase engagement. A campaign is an organized marketing operation with defined achievements in a specific area to meet an overall objective. Keyword placement, timing, and sharing social currency are the most effective techniques.

Social Media Marketing (SMM) is driving traffic to a website from social media. Word of user marketing has higher brand value than paid advertising because we trust our friends opinions. SMM tactics include, PPC advertising, keyword optimization, branding, and A/B Testing.

Brand

A brand is a product, service, or organization with a distinct design recognized by their consumers. It is the collection of images that represent an organization.

Branding distinguishes a brand from others through advertising and design. Brands gain recognition in the mind of consumers by differentiating from similar things.

Formulas

MDS formulas are used to help make good business decisions. They provide KPI's or other ratios and comparable numbers for analysis.

A ratio is a relationship between numbers. They measure the number of times one value can be divided into another. The comparison is expressed as a percentage or rate.

Click Through Rate

Click Through Rate (CTR) is a ratio that displays the percentage of website visitors who click on an advertisement or hyperlink compared to the total number of times it is viewed. Views are sometimes called impressions for advertisements.

CTR = Clicks / Views

Referral Rate

The referral rate is a ratio that displays the percentage of total website traffic from a given hyperlink. The number of clicks to a website divided by the total visitors to a website for a given time period. The bounce rate is a referral rate for a landing page.

RR = Clicks / Visitors

Return On Investment (ROI)

Return On Investment (ROI) is the incremental revenue contribution from media expenditures like search engine and keyword purchase. The net value of incremental revenue generated by the media purchase less the variable cost of producing that revenue, including the media cost.

ROI = Revenue Increase − Variable Cost

Cost Per Click

Cost Per Click (CPC) is the total cost of a marketing campaign divided by the number of clicks received through the site where the campaign was targeted.

CPC = Cost / Clicks

Email rules are highly developed because it is the oldest form of online communication. The guidelines are highly developed as well. There are technical aspects we should know about. Understanding is part of effective communication because it is asynchronous.

Email Rules

- Send messages during normal hours or it may call your lifestyle into question.
- Sign messages because it gives them credibility.
- Write short messages because people do not read an entire message when it is long.
- Ask before sending attachments because many servers block attachments and large files.
- Refrain from sharing addresses of others without permission because they are personal information.

- Use a descriptive subject line to ensure it gets read because we delete messages based on subject.
- Tell the recipient if the message is long in the subject because it may get deleted otherwise.

Guidelines

Subject

The Subject of an email displays in the inbox of a recipient. 50 characters are visible on desktop computers. 25 on smartphones. Approximately half of all email is consumed on a phone. There is more of a chance it will be read if the whole subject is viewed.

Writing the subject line first to gives the content context as it is written. Describe the topic, set a deadline if applicable, and do not include filler words.

Inbox Zero

Inbox zero is a term that describes an email account without any messages in the inbox. It is empty because messages are completed and deleted. Those that cannot be acted upon immediately are replied to and put in appropriate folders.

Deleting incoming messages based on subject line and sender is done frequently. Folders are created to classify requests. Some are created for read only mail.

Addressing Email

The "To:" field is for the addresses of those directly addressed in the message. Those who shall act on the information.

The "CC:" field is for those indirectly addressed in the message. A carbon copy (cc) for their own information. They need to know the information but not necessarily act upon it.

The "BCC:" field is used to address multiple people. It is for protecting the privacy of recipients when sending mass messages and newsletters. A blind carbon copy that only shows the email address of the person who receives it even though the message is sent to many people. It is a common courtesy to use this field when sending a message to multiple people.

Inverted Pyramid

The Inverted Pyramid is a journalistic style of writing whose structure prioritizes the placement of information within the content. Information is placed by order of importance to the reader. The most important information comes first.

Email

Email is an electronic message sent to and from an internet domain. We send messages through the internet in various file formats to unique addresses. One to one and one to many communication is available.

Simple Mail Transfer Protocol (SMTP) is the name used to describe the set of computer network standards used for sending and receiving email messages with an email server.

Post Office Protocol Version 3 (Pop3) is a set of computer network standards used for downloading messages from an email server to a computer. It may be used with SMTP. SMTP is not required. It is compatible.

Internet Message Access Protocol (IMAP) is a standard for downloading email messages from a server.

Spoofing

A spoof email message is one that has been altered to imitate an authentic message. It is a hoax because automatic header information is manually changed to a different email address than that of the originator of the message.

Catch All

Domains allow webmasters to create catch all email addresses. Catch all email addresses receive the messages of all specified addresses within a domain. Creating an email address to forward messages to another one can be done by adjusting the settings on any email account or by a webmaster creating a catch-all email account within a domain.

Spam

Spam is unwanted email. The most common form is email advertising. Typically, a large number of marketing messages are sent to addresses without authorization. Email applications filter bulk email into a spam folder.

Signature

An email signature is a block of text at the end of a message used to help determine message authenticity. The senders name and contact information is included as evidence of authenticity.

It may be automatically inserted. A file containing the text block is added to the message. The sender must create the file. It is a feature of most accounts that can be turned on or off.

Attachments

An attachment is an extra part of a document. Files are added to messages as a supplement. Image, pdf, and zipped files are common. Executable programs are blocked by antivirus software to prevent being hacked.

Personal Email

Personal email is for sharing good news and essential information. It is used effectively for scheduling and announcements. Electronic greeting cards and invitations are common.

Professional Email

Professional email messages are about how we earn a living. It is an essential tool for most professionals. Instructions are often given to employees through email.

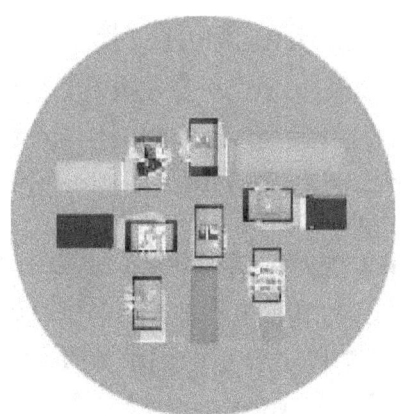

Software

An email client is Mail User Agent (MUA) software used to manage accounts. It is groupware because messaging allows people to work together remotely. There is a large market.

Basic features are the same. Most allow multiple account management. Mobile and desktop are separate market segments with little overlap.

Correspondence

Exchanging email messages is more formal than text, forum, or chat. It is similar to a letter sent through the mail. The layout does not resemble a formal letter in most cases. Signatures are the most formal part. Most people are comfortable with this type of communication including its asynchronicity.

There are many things that can prevent a reply. Messages are often deleted by mistake. Spam folders filter incoming mail that is not spam. Recipients may not check their inbox regularly. They may be too busy to reply.

We are comfortable with email. There are many conventions. The amount of time spent using it will likely increase with informatization.

Video rules include watching and creating it. The guidelines are for making video. Explanations provide an understanding of the technology. We are comfortable with the medium given its popularity.

Video Rules

- Use earphones in public to avoid disturbing those around you.
- Post positive comments and like because it encourages more production of that type.
- Use moderation when uploading or watching human violence because it teaches it.
- Provide constructive criticism because we may not know how to improve without it.
- Credit sources because content without attribution or right may be infringement.

- Watch responsibly because graphic content may have redeeming qualities and children have to be protected.

Guidelines

Lighting

The lighter the better. Outdoor shooting can be one with the sun behind the camera for good light. A lot of backlighting can make centered people glow.

Rule of Thirds

A shot is divided equally in thirds from top to bottom and left to right. There is an imaginary grid. The intersections of lines are the focal points for our eyes. They are slightly off center to the right, left, up, and down.

Shots may look more appealing when subjects are at focal points. Centered shots may place important characteristics at focal points. Centering according to the grid instead of object.

B Roll

B Roll is additional video shot to supplement the main content of a story. It is edited into the content. In camera edits are shots made by stopping and starting the camera in sequence. Post production editing shots can be taken out of sequence.

Video

Film is a term that denotes the movie industry. A movie is a sequence of recorded visual images captured by a camera transmitted to a screen that appear to be in motion. A motion picture. Video is another name for the recording.

Internet video is digital video. A digital format for the delivery of motion pictures that uses 0's and 1's to represent the data. Motion pictures delivered through the internet to a screen for display.

Watch time determines the value because it measures engagement. Some people believe complete viewing is required. Watch time can be used for analysis in making it better.

Subscribers watch videos more than anyone else. Descriptions influence readers and search engines. Compatibility determines viewing capability.

Storytelling

Storytelling is a principle of video. It is an account of real or imagined events communicated for entertainment purposes.

Subscribers

An internet subscriber is a user who is notified of new video publications by a creator by signing up.

Description

A video description is a text based account of the genre, publication date, and plot that accompany video transmitted through the internet.

Compatibility

Compatibility allows one computer, file, or software program to be used with another. Computers, files, and software that are compatible work with each other.

Premium

Premium video content is professionally produced. It is delivered on Demand for free and through paid subscriptions in streams.

Television networks provide streams of current shows online. Past seasons generally require a subscription. Reseller networks may have episodes on Demand. Networks provide films on Demand and with subscriptions.

Social

Social video is UGC. It is a form of social media. Networks for sharing it are popular. It is popular in all forms of social media. Content creators range from amateur to semi-professional all the way up to professional production company. The majority of accounts are amateurs who watch video with the ability to upload if they choose.

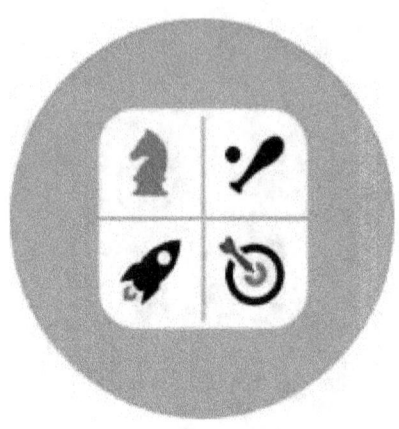

Video Game

Video games are stories that require user input in the manipulation of images on a screen for a desired outcome. The desired outcome is a competitive goal. Players compete according to set rules against the program and other players. They can be played on computers, dedicated consoles, or other electronics.

Entertainment Console

An entertainment console is a media player that outputs electronic signals to televisions or monitors for display. Video Game Consoles, Digital Versatile Disc (DVD) Players, and Streaming devices are entertainment consoles. Most video game consoles include DVD Players and streaming services.

Mobile Video

Mobile Video is the wireless transfer of video content to a device that can be easily moved. Streaming motion pictures from a hotspot router or wireless carrier makes video mobile. The process uses a lot of data. High Definition (HD) uses an extremely large amount of data.

Appendix A

Keyword Research
Keyword.io: http://www.keyword.io

Social Mention (Hashtags & Keywords): http://www.socialmention.com

Content Marketing
Alltop: http://www.alltop.com

Buzz Sumo: http://www.buzzsumo.com

Social Media Monitoring & Research
FollowerWonk: http://ww.followerwonk.com

Buzz Sumo: http://www.buzzsumo.com

SocialBro: http://www.socialbro.com

Link Shorteners
Bitly: https://bitly.com/

Google: https://goo.gl/

Social Media Managers
HootSuite: https://hootsuite.com/

Buffer: https://buffer.com/

Friends+Me: https://friendsplus.me/

Browsers
Chrome:
https://www.google.com/intl/en/chrome/browser/desktop/index.html

Opera: http://www.opera.com/

Firefox: https://www.mozilla.org/en-US/firefox/products/

Cloud Storage
Google Drive: https://www.google.com/drive/

One Drive:
https://onedrive.live.com/about/en-us/

Dropbox: https://www.dropbox.com

Productivity Software
Microsoft Office Online:
https://office.live.com/

Google Docs:
https://www.google.com/docs/about/

OpenOffice: https://www.openoffice.org/

Email
Gmail:
https://www.google.com/intl/en/mail/help/about.html

Outlook.com: http://www.live.com

Yahoo Mail:
https://login.yahoo.com/config/mail

Tutorials
Howcast: http://www.howcast.com/

The Google Play Store is the standard for all Apps because Android is the most popular Operating System (OS). The categories contained in it encompass the categories of the smaller stores and eclipse them. Therefore, I have provided a description of each category in the Google Play Store. The categories are common to all App Stores.

Categories:

Books and Reference

A reference App is a software program that acts as a point of contact for information about a topic or subject. Books and Reference Apps include readers, dictionaries, popular book, and niche informational Apps. Reader devices have Apps so that content can be displayed on other devices. Popular books have their own Apps and various subjects have them as well.

Business

A business App is a software program that assists you in a commercial or mercantile activity. Business Apps are mostly productivity Apps that cost money and other Apps for communication and delivery.

Comics

A comic book App is a software program that is an e-reader to display a series of drawings that tell a funny story. The type of humor in a given App varies greatly. Some Apps focus on humor types, while others focus on particular characters and stories. There are various writing and drawing styles available in comic Apps.

Communication

Communication Apps are software programs for the transmissions from one person or entity to another. Wi-Fi hotspot Apps, email, and Voice over IP (VoIP) are common communication Apps. Web browsers are included in this category as well.

Education

Education Apps are software programs that assist in the dissemination of accumulated knowledge about a particular subject to an individual. Education apps include kids learning games and guides. Education websites have Apps for interaction with their site from a mobile device. Online learning platforms have Apps so that students can connect with their online classes.

Entertainment

Entertainment Apps are software programs for amusement that engage users to watch, listen, or play games. Entertainment Apps include radio, television, and video Apps. Most are players of some sort for streaming media.

Finance

Finance Apps are software programs designed to help you save money. Many finance Apps track spending in various ways, budget resources, and balance checkbooks. Banks, credit card companies, and online payment services have Apps in the finance category as well.

Health & Fitness

Health and fitness Apps are software programs that help you achieve and maintain a sound mind, body, and spirit. There are many exercise Apps in the health and fitness category. Heart rate checkers, calorie counters, and weight loss Apps are popular as well.

Libraries & Demo

Libraries and demo Apps are software programs that connect you to content for use. Demo Apps are trial software available for a limited time with limited functionality. There are many language, sound, and undefined Apps in the library and demo section.

Lifestyle

Lifestyle Apps are software programs that assist you in your way of life. Food, recipe, and relationship Apps are common in this category. There are alarm clock, restaurant, and fast food Apps.

Live Wallpaper

Live wallpaper Apps are software programs that decorate the background of the screen on your mobile device. Many live wallpaper Apps feature objects that move in the background. 3D, thematic, and picture wallpaper Apps are common in this category.

Media and Video

Media and video Apps are software programs that assist you in watching and creating pictures, sound, and text together or separately. Video players, editors, and camera monitoring system Apps are all included in the media and video category. Ring-tone makers have Apps in this section. Video websites and television stations provide Apps for their content in this category as well.

Medical

Medical Apps are software programs that help you maintain your health and alleviate ailments. There are a lot of diagnosis, pregnancy, and first aid Apps in the medical section. Blood pressure, drug, and charting Apps are popular as well.

Music and Audio

Music and audio Apps are software programs that play and record sounds including vocals and instrumentals. Music player and voice recorders are the most popular Apps in the music and audio section. Free and premium streaming music providers have Apps in this category as well.

News and Magazine

News and magazine Apps are software programs that provide reports about recent events, various topics, and other facts. Newspapers, television stations, and subscription magazines have Apps in the news and magazine section. There are many niche

Apps for reports about various subjects as well, that include politics among other things.

Personalization

Personalization Apps are software programs that help you mark your mobile device in a way particular to you and your liking. Wallpaper, screensaver locks, and widget Apps are included in the personalization category. Ring-tone and special font Short Messaging Service (SMS) Apps can be found in the personalization category as well.

Photography

Photography Apps are software programs that control the camera of a mobile device and manipulate the data of pictures. There are many different camera Apps available for a wide variety of purposes that range from high definition and video to special effects and fast bursts of pictures. Photo editing and picture social networking Apps can be found in the photography category as well.

Productivity

Productivity Apps are software programs that help you create, store, and organize as a category in the App Store. The strict definition of productivity software is different. Note taking, calendar, password protector, and reader Apps are popular in the productivity category. Printing, scanning, and other document creating Apps can be found in the productivity category as well.

Shopping

Shopping Apps are software programs that assist you in the purchase of good and services. Ecommerce websites, store, and sale locator, and list Apps are popular shopping Apps. Retail stores have Apps in the shopping section. Barcode scanners and comparison Apps are in the shopping section as well.

Social

Social Apps are software programs that connect you with your friends and help you communicate. Social networks have their

Apps in the social category. Many social networking organizational Apps can be found here as well.

Sports

Sports Apps are software programs designed to assist you in individual and team competition and give reports about them. Popular sport leagues and news and television channels have Apps for reporting scores and showing highlights. There are many Apps that coach players and assist coaches with tips and by capturing video in this section. Golf has many popular Apps.

Tools

Tool Apps are software programs designed for a particular task in your mobile device or that allow you to perform a task with your mobile device. Data backup, flashlight, and screenshot Apps are the most popular in the tools category. Anti-virus and keyboard Apps can be found here as well. This category in the

App Store is a slight variation of the strict definition of tools software.

Transportation

Transportation Apps are software programs designed to help you move yourself or something from one place to another. Car finding, speed trap locator, and auto unlock Apps are very popular in this category. GPS tracking, rental car, and bus schedule Apps can be found in the transportation category as well.

Travel & Local

Travel and local Apps are software programs designed to help you make a journey. Flight tracker, map, and navigation Apps are the most popular travel Apps. Airlines, hotels, and booking services all have Apps in the travel section.

Weather

Weather Apps are designed to report and predict the state of the atmosphere and its condition. Various weather services provide Apps in the weather section. Radar weather forecasting Apps are available as well.

Widgets

Widget Apps are software programs designed to enable you to perform or access a service. There are a variety of Apps from all categories in this section because widgets are used by many of them to allow you to access them. All popular Apps have widgets. This section is a good place to look for popular Apps.

World Wide Web Consortium (W3C)

When something is popular enough to have an acronym named after it, it is a principle. Most people agree about what it is or does. The World Wide Web Consortium is known by the acronym W3C.

The W3C is the most widely recognized standards board for internet transmission. It was started in 1994. It is the standard resource for web programmers using HTML and CSS.

The organization periodically releases new standards for web design and development. The current standard is HTML5 and CSS3. These are the fundamental programming languages used to display web pages. Use the W3C standards for programming websites.

Web pages can be made without using the W3C standards because they are displayed in software programs called browsers. Browsers interpret HTML according to their own standards. Each one is a little different. They display code that is not HTML.

The following code is the basic HTML5 syntax for creating a website to be displayed on the internet. In principle, this is all you need to master to be a web designer or developer because all tags are defined by the W3C. A tag is the data between the brackets, <>. Everything beyond this basic code can be found on their website.

Copy the code into a notepad document or other HTML editor. Save it with the letters html after the file name and a period, filename.hmtl. Click to open from a file manager. Make sure the quotes are straight rather than curly.

Open Graph
```
<meta property="og:title"
content="Netiquette" />

<meta property="og:type" content="website"
/>
```

```
<meta property="og:url"
content="http://www.networketiquette.net"
/>

<meta property="og:image"
content="http://www.networketiquette.net/i
mages/netiquette_sign_logo.png" />

<meta property="og:site_name"
content="Netiquette" />

<meta property="og:video"
content="http://youtu.be/bH8r_H9N9T4" />

<meta property="og:description"
content="Netiquette is the social code of the
internet. The rules are common conventions
internet communication." />
```